The Heart of Wakefield Project

In 2015, Wakefield Council invited Wakefield Civic Society, Wakefield Historical Society and Leeds Beckett University to join The Heart of Wakefield Project. This project was set up to undertake research into the history of the Wood Street area and to promote an interest in that history to the wider community, including local residents, businesses, school children and students as well as to visitors to the city.

A partnership was formed and a successful bid was made to the Heritage Lottery Fund for funding to cover the costs of the project. Working with Faceless Arts Company and One to One Development Trust, outreach activities were undertaken to engage the community in a number of investigative and creative endeavours to produce original research, artwork and other material to deepen our understanding of the rich heritage of the street and its buildings. This book is just one of the outputs from the project. In due course, the Civic Society will be erecting some new blue plaques along the street and offering a number of tailored guided walks and talks. Meanwhile, Wakefield Historical Society will be continuing with research and creating a repository of information and images while students from Leeds Beckett University are working on an on-line map of the area.

Almost inevitably, a publication of this sort can only capture a snapshot in time: as with any street, people come and people go, businesses arrive and depart and buildings change, some being modified over time, others being demolished altogether to be replaced with new ones on the same site. As our research continues, our understanding of the history of the street also changes: new characters emerge, old events are discovered, and memories are jogged.

In writing this book, I have tried to convey a flavour of the history of what is now one of Wakefield's most important, and imposing, streets – a street that has been the location of administration and law for not only Wakefield but, in its day, the wider West Riding (and later West Yorkshire) area. I am indebted to our partners and other contributors to the project who have done most of the research and to the historians, writers and photographers who have produced much of the previously published work on the history of our city. Without their invaluable efforts and the ongoing work being done by Wakefield Historical Society in particular, this book could not have been written.

Kevin Trickett,

President, Wakefield Civic Society

May 2017

Contents

Wakefield's Market Cross from a print by the Rev. Thomas Kilby, Wakefield Council Libraries Photographic Collection

Heart of Wakefield

Wood Street, 1953. Note the bunting – 1953 was Coronation Year; the zebra crossing and the traffic lights – one of only two sets in the city centre at that time (the other being on the junction of Leigh Street with Kirkgate). Photo Copyright The Francis Frith Collection

Before Wood Street

Today, Wakefield, which became a city in 1888, is a mix of modern and historic buildings and, like all cities, it continues to evolve. However, despite the many modern developments, it is a city in which much of the mediaeval street pattern can still be traced.

Look at an old map of Wakefield created before 1800 and you'll struggle to find Wood Street: it simply wasn't there! Although the city of Wakefield can trace its history back to pre-Norman times, Wood Street itself is relatively recent and dates from around the beginning of the 19th Century. To understand why Wood Street exists (and how it acquired its name!), we first need to examine a little of Wakefield's earlier history.

In mediaeval times, the centre of Wakefield had three principal streets – Northgate, Westgate and Kirkgate (the suffix 'gate' is derived from the old Norse – or Viking – word 'gata', meaning street). The land on either side of these streets was divided up into plots of land, known as burgage plots; ribbons of land that had a relatively narrow frontage but which stretched back some way from the street to provide smallholdings on which tenants (and, later, owners) could build their outbuildings, grow produce and maybe even keep animals . This 'toft and croft' arrangement – where the plot of land consisted of a house with a small rear yard (the toft) behind which was an area where produce could be grown (the croft) – was a familiar arrangement in many towns and villages.

Wood Street in the early 1930s –
Wakefield Council Libraries Photographic Collection

These burgage plots were developed over time; businesses sprang up; more dwellings and other outbuildings were added. To maximise the potential use of the land, access from the main street would be provided, usually wide enough perhaps for a horse and cart to move along, or in the grander buildings, horses and carriages.

This development gave rise to the pattern of yards that can still be traced in some parts of the city today, particularly along Westgate but also, albeit to a lesser extent, in Northgate, Kirkgate and elsewhere: parallel strips of development running back from the main street.

It is thought that there might have been as many as 150 of these yards by the 1920s although counting them with certainty has proved difficult for historians as the names of the yards, often derived from the names of families or businesses, particularly inns, tended to change if the family or business moved.

A good number of the yards have since been opened up into streets in their own right while others have been swept away altogether as part of the ongoing regeneration of the city centre. Sadly, at least for the purposes of this book, even where the yards remain, many of their original buildings have been demolished as part of the slum clearances of the 1930s and later.

Often lacking in sanitation and ventilation, being overcrowded and densely packed together, with people and animals living in close proximity, the yards were hardly the healthiest places in which to live – as 19th century outbreaks of cholera and other epidemics, such as smallpox, testify. Dwellings were frequently damp, filthy and, most likely, noisy. It is no wonder, therefore, that people with the resources to do so, moved out of the town centre in search of more gentrified company in the open countryside.

The area around today's St John's was, in the late 18th and early 19th centuries, one such place of relative tranquillity and refinement. Some half-mile or more from the hustle and bustle of the town centre, and prior to the commencement of development, the area consisted mainly of fields and allotments for the growing of produce. The location was elevated and offered fresher air and purpose-built living accommodation was to be provided by local lawyer and property developer John Lee (1759-1836), keen to tempt new residents to move there.

Lee was, in effect, what we would regard today as a property speculator. Aside from his legal practice, but no doubt hand in hand with it, and in partnership with his business associate Wakefield wool merchant Francis Maude who was able to provide financial backing, Lee had been buying up plots of land in and around the town centre. With Maude, he had managed to acquire large tracts in what was then known as the Cliff Field (so called because it was atop a piece of elevated land which fell away sharply – the Cliff – to the west and north) but which we now know as St John's. This land was ripe for future development – all that was needed was the opportunity!

A Chapel of Ease – the development of St John's Church

The decision to build a new church (St John's) at the top end of Northgate was in part brought about by a need to ease pressure on the parish church (today's Cathedral) which was struggling to cope with a growing congregation (the population of Wakefield being some 8,000 or thereabouts at the turn of the 18th century), and partly through opportunity: Lee and Maude had a suitable site at their disposal!

So, when a public meeting held at the parish church in 1788 agreed that a new church should be built, Lee and Maude were able to offer the project a plot of land. They were appointed as two of the trustees responsible for taking the project forward, something which involved raising funds and obtaining parliamentary approval (granted in 1791).

The church was built to a design by architects William Lindley and Charles Watson. The foundation stone was laid in November 1791 and the church was consecrated on 28th July 1795. Funds were raised by public subscription and from the sale of pews on which the owner was allowed to charge rent (Lee being one of the people who purchased such pews).

St John's was the first Anglican church to be built in Wakefield since the time of Henry VIII and the Reformation. Its tower contributes to the distinctive Wakefield skyline, adding to the architectural line-up up of the spire of the Cathedral, the tower of the Town Hall and the cupola of County Hall.

(Since its completion, the church has undergone a number of physical changes and internal re-orderings, the most significant of which was undertaken under the supervision of Wakefield-born architect John Micklethwaite in the late 19th century.)

The church was originally approached via a new road from Northgate along which Lee and Maude began building a terrace of new houses. This was to be called St John's Street (St John's North today). Lee financed the houses to the west of the street (nearest the church) while he and Maude sold the rest of the plots on the east end of the street, including the site of what was to be the central house, to local builder William Puckrin, painter George Bennett and joiner Robert Lee. To ensure uniformity of design, the design of the fronts was under the management of architect John Thompson of Wakefield. The row was completed by 1796.

Having bought Maude out, Lee went on to develop the houses along the north and west sides of what is today St John's Square but which was originally called St John's Place. Again, to ensure uniformity, Lee engaged architect Charles Watson to design the fronts but purchasers were allowed greater freedom around the back – hence the disparity in design quality at the rear of the properties. The Square was completed by around 1803 – although, it should be noted, there were never any plans to add a south side.

(For more information about John Lee, including his venture to develop St John's, see **Attorney At Large**, John Goodchild, 1986, published by Wakefield Historical Publications.)

St John's Church today

A New Street To A New Town

As we have seen, St John's Square was at the time some half mile remote from the built-up town centre. It was in essence a 'new town' development enjoying an elevated and almost rural aspect. The main route to the area from the town was via Northgate while journeys to the north were via Leeds and then Bradford Roads, both of which were turnpikes (or toll roads). Bradford Road connected with Leeds Road at Newton Bar but Lee was a trustee of the Bradford and Wakefield Turnpike and was charged with entering into negotiations to extend the road up to and through St John's towards Back Lane.

The opening up of new roads and the development of St John's in turn seems to have catalysed other developments by other land owners and, in short succession, new roads such as Bond Street, Burton Street and Bell Street were laid out to the south of St John's.

One such development was the opening up of land behind the Angel Inn in 1806 to create a new street. The land was owned by the Reverend William Wood of Woodthorpe, a client of John Lee and the second vicar of St John's Church (from 1805 to 1825). Wood was not averse to a little property development and speculation in his own right!

Have a look at the map to the right, reproduced here with the kind permission of West Yorkshire Archive Service.

It was drawn in the 1790s and shows the Wakefield enclosures. Northgate is the broad band curving up from the bottom right-hand corner of the picture. The road which branches off to the lower left is what today we know as The Bull Ring and Marygate, just before it merges with Westgate. The land on each side of the main streets is divided up into (burgage) plots and each plot is marked with a number. Pay particular attention to the plots numbered 763 and 764. At the time of the Wakefield Enclosures Act of 1793, the ownership of these plots was shown as follows: plot no. 763 is recorded as being owned freehold by the above Rev. Wood and consists of several 'messuages' (i.e., a dwelling house possibly with outbuildings), and The Angel Inn. Meanwhile, lot 764 is shown as being owned freehold by George John Lee Esq, a relative of John Lee. This smaller lot consisted of one messuage, outbuildings and yard, including the White Lion Public House (presumably the messuage in question).

The Rev. Wood demolished the Angel Inn and laid out a new road, which he named after himself, connecting the Bull Ring (formerly known as the Market Place) with the newly laid out Bond Street. He then divided the land up into development plots, selling a chunk of land at the north end to the West Riding Magistrates to enable the building of a new court house there. This was to be the first 'civic' building in the street – although the original intention had been to build the Court House closer to the House of Correction.

Work on the Court House, built in the Greek Revival style to a design by Charles Watson, commenced in 1806 and was completed in 1810 (although the building was extended in 1849-50 and again in the 1880s).

So, there we have the makings of Wood Street. Other buildings followed, of course, including other civic buildings such as the Town Hall, police stations, health offices and a museum, as well as a post office and a hospital, shops, offices, hotels and banks.

We will now take a look at the history of some of those buildings but will leave the stories of the, often unexpected, events such as riots and civil commotions, the flying of hot air balloons, the firing of cannon, the arrival of visiting circuses and many other stories for another day.

1790s enclosures map of what was to become the Wood Street area. Courtesy of West Yorkshire Archive Service (File No. Vol 4/28) and with thanks to Lesley Taylor, a member of both Wakefield Civic and Wakefield Historical Societies for researching this

Taken from a print by the Reverend Thomas Kilby (1796-1868), the third incumbent of St John's Church (from 1825 to 1868), this picture looks up towards St John's Church from the north end of Wood Street. The building that appears to the left of the tower is the former residence of JW Walker, historian and author of *Wakefield: Its History and People*. It later became the school dental clinic and then part of Wakefield College. It was demolished in August and September 2011 as part of the redevelopment of the College campus. The wall and trees to the far left of the picture surround Rishworth House – the site of County Hall today. Illustration courtesy Wakefield Council Libraries Photographic Collection

This illustration, another one taken from a print by the Reverend Thomas Kilby, shows Wood Street in the mid-nineteenth century with the Court House to the right of the picture. Beyond the Court House is the Mechanics' Institute – note that there is no Town Hall (this was built in 1880).

Opposite the Court House is the site of the Paragon Iron Foundry. Further down the street, the tall building is the Royal Hotel, formerly The Woodman Inn. Illustration courtesy Wakefield Council Libraries Photographic Collection

A Centre for Administration

By the early 19th century, the administration of what was then the Manor of Wakefield was in the hands of a number of groups and individuals - Constables, Stewards, Ale-Tasters, Pindars, Street Commissioners and a Board of Guardians amongst them, but overall responsibility lay with the Magistracy. Democracy, such as it was, was played out through public meetings to discuss matters of the day. These meetings were called by petition to the Constable and took place in the Manorial Moot Hall, among other venues, which stood in Manor House Yard, off upper Kirkgate (where Boots is today).

The magistrates, meanwhile, met in rooms at the White Hart Hotel (on the corner of Upper Kirkgate and Southgate opposite the tower end of the Cathedral) until the opening of their new Court House in Wood Street in 1810, while the Street Commissioners, responsible for such things as sanitation and street lighting, met in a chamber above the Market Cross in Cross Square (near today's Black Rock public house).

The passing of the Municipal Corporations Act in 1835 allowed for the creation of municipal boroughs administered by locally elected councillors. These municipal boroughs, organised along standardised lines, replaced the rather ad hoc arrangements for local governance described above that had existed not only in Wakefield but across the country since the middle ages.

Towns had to petition the government for incorporation and Wakefield became a municipal borough in 1848 although the Street Commissioners retained much of their power to begin with. With incorporation came the first elected council whose members gradually took on the responsibilities for such things as sanitation, policing, street lighting and planning. The Street Commissioners held their final meeting in the chamber above the Market Cross, in 1853. The building was demolished in 1866 as it was deemed to be impeding trade for shopkeepers. Meanwhile, the new council started to look for premises from which to conduct the administration of the town, as Wakefield still was.

Artwork by Faceless and the people of Wakefield

The Market Cross

The building, which was paid for by public subscription, was erected in 1707 during the reign of Queen Anne at the top end of Cross Square. It consisted of eight Doric pillars supporting a chamber above under a domed roof with a lantern above and topped off with a weather vane. The chamber was reached by a spiral staircase and provided a meeting room for the Street Commissioners and others.

In the space between the pillars, market traders would sell their fresh farm produce such as butter, eggs and poultry.

The shop keepers in Cross Square eventually took against the building and petitioned for its demolition. Despite public opposition, this was agreed by the Corporation, albeit with only a narrow vote in favour, and demolition was begun on 19th September 1866. Materials were sold off and some of the pillars went to local houses such as Clarke Hall (where they are still used to support the roof of the loggia in the garden to the rear of the property). One of the columns can be seen in the Secret Garden at Thornes Park.

Note that the picture shows a building behind the Market Cross, appearing to close off the southern end of Cross Square. In fact, a narrow passageway to the left of the Square, known as The Shambles, or Butchers' Row, connected the Square with what was then known as Great Passage but is now an extension of Northgate.

Wakefield's Market Cross from a print by the Rev. Thomas Kilby, Wakefield Council Libraries Photographic Collection

Standing in Crown Court (between Wood Street and King Street), the 'old' Town Hall (the second building from the left) is now offices and apartments. Photo: John Bickerdike, Wakefield Civic Society

Two Town Halls

The new municipal corporation held their meetings in either the Public Rooms in Wood Street or in the Court House, and also in rented offices in Barstow Square but began to realise that they would need permanent premises of their own. When the Public Rooms were put up for sale in 1855, the Corporation was urged to acquire them for use as a Town Hall but it was not to be and the building was purchased by the Mechanics' Institute

In 1854, the Corporation purchased a plot of land in Wood Street that had previously been the site of a stone quarry but which had been filled in and levelled to create a vegetable market there. In the end, the market did not proceed and the land was sold by the owner to the Corporation which had the intention of building the Town Hall on the site. However, having acquired the site, the Corporation did nothing with it for some twenty years, concerned about how to cover the building costs – a suggestion that the cost be covered by a charge on the rates led to an outcry and a public meeting held in the Court House made clear the opposition to the scheme.

Instead of building a new Town Hall, the Corporation was therefore obliged to seek rental premises. They entered into negotiations with Jonathan Bayldon, the owner of the former Assembly Rooms in Crown Court (between King Street and Wood Street) to move into his premises as tenants. This building, erected in in 1778 and sometimes referred to as the Music Hall, had been used for a variety of purposes and Wakefield's *The Wakefield Star,* established in 1803, was also published

from there. From 1845 to 1858 the Wakefield Church Institution used a part of the building for its library, lectures and evening classes. However, there was a fire in 1858 which badly damaged the building.

Wakefield Corporation paid the building's owner to rebuild and refurbish it to meet their needs and the new council moved there in 1861, the Church Institution having moved to a new building of their own in Marygate. This was, then, to become Wakefield's first Town Hall (the words are still carved into the stone pediment above the entrance).

However, this could only be a stop-gap arrangement and it was not long before the Corporation realised they would need somewhere bigger and purpose-built to better meet their needs. Not only that, but they wanted something more suited to the dignity of the Corporation and which could hold its own in comparison to the town halls of neighbouring towns.

The Corporation had acquired the Tammy Hall in 1875. The Hall was around twice its current length and the Corporation demolished part of it to create a larger building site in Wood Street for the new Town Hall they wished to build. What was left of the Tammy Hall was converted into a fire and police station.

In 1877, the Corporation committed at last to a project to build a Town Hall befitting the town. An architectural competition was advertised to select a design and this was won by London architect Thomas Colcutt.

Thomas Colcutt (1840-1924) was also the architect for both the Savoy Hotel and the Palace Theatre in London.

Building work started in October 1877 with the laying of the foundation stone by the mayor, Alderman WH Gill.

Three years later, in October 1880, the Town Hall was officially opened by that year's mayor, WH Lee. The streets on either side of the building are, perhaps fittingly, named Gill Street and Lee Street.

Opinions seem to differ as to how to describe the architectural style of the building – Gothic, free Tudor, English (or possibly French) Renaissance, and Jacobean. Whatever the style, the building is now Grade I listed and so we can turn to the 'official listing' on the Historic England website for advice.

In so doing, we see that the building is designed in "a freely-interpreted north European Gothic style with Jacobean decorative touches" and with "Very steeply pitched Welsh slate roofs having ornamental shaped and pedimented gable ends and tall, many-shafted chimneys." That will do for us!

The gates across the main entrance bear Wakefield's original coat of arms, the Fleur de Lys, and the emblem of Yorkshire, the White Rose.

The Town Hall is built in Ashlar stone in narrow, irregular courses with a tower that is 45.4 metres high (149 feet). The bell weighs 2.7 tonnes and, as local residents will testify, can be clearly heard right across the city!

In 2014/15, the Town Hall underwent an extensive refurbishment. As well as being home to Wakefield Council, the Town Hall now also accommodates the Register Office and Wakefield Civic Society, both located on the ground floor.

The Town Hall. Photo: John Bickerdike, Wakefield Civic Society

The County Hall

Although not strictly speaking on Wood Street, it would be remiss not to say something about County Hall which dominates the north end of the street.

The West Riding County Council (WRCC) was created in 1889 as a result of the Local Government Act of the year before. The Council was based in Wakefield and at first shared premises at the new Town Hall in Wood Street with Wakefield Council. However, the building was not large enough to accommodate both administrations and the WRCC commissioned premises of their own. The WRCC had already acquired Rishworth House – a large Georgian House built by Wakefield banker Thomas Rishworth. The house had been purchased by the Magistrates to use as offices and meeting rooms as well as a residence for the Deputy Clerk. While consideration was given to using the house for the new County Council, and locations in other towns were also explored, it was decided that the WRCC should remain in Wakefield and that Rishworth House should be demolished to create a site for what was to become the County Hall.

As with Wakefield's Town Hall, an architectural competition was announced and the winning design was by James Gibson and Samuel Russell of Grays Inn Square, London. Building commenced in 1894 and the building was opened by the Marquess of Ripon on 22nd February 1898. A decision was made early on to install electricity even though there was no actual supply when building work began but no doubt in the knowledge that it would come – as it did in 1896.

The building was extended in 1910-14 along Burton Street.

The County Hall. Photo: John Bickerdike, Wakefield Civic Society

The Court House

As we have seen, this was the first of the 'civic' buildings in Wood Street, opening in 1810. It was where the West Riding County Quarter Sessions were held – courts that met quarterly to consider more serious criminal cases. But they also made decisions on civil matters such as roads and bridge repairs, licensing and county police matters. Quarter Sessions were abolished in 1972 under an act of Parliament. Like the Quarter Sessions, earlier meetings of the Petty Sessions would have been held at the White Hart. After the creation of the Municipal Borough and the building of the Town Hall, there were separate Petty Sessions for the Borough in the Town Hall, while Petty Sessions for the County continued to be held in the Court House. The Court House also provided a large open space that was used for public meetings as well as court business. It closed in 1993 when the work of the court was transferred to Leeds and the building was sold.

In 2013, after many years of standing empty, the Grade II* building was entered onto the English Heritage (now Historic England) 'Buildings at Risk' register. It has since been purchased by Wakefield Council and awaits repair and a new use. (Note the phone box in the picture right is also listed Grade II!)

Artwork by Faceless and the people of Wakefield

Tammy Hall

From mediaeval times, the textile industry provided Wakefield with one of its principal sources of income. From its capacity to weave its own woollen cloths through to dyeing and finishing cloths for others, Wakefield became an important centre for the wool trade and wool staplers' warehouses stood side by side with warehouses storing grain across the town, from the waterfront right up into the town centre.

One trade to be established successfully, if briefly, in the town was the trade in tammies and camlets, types of durable worsted cloth, sometimes glazed. Such was the demand that local merchants decided to build a hall for the sale of such goods. The Tammy Hall was erected on land bought by a group of merchants off Back Lane and was opened for business in 1778. Containing some 200 stalls over two floors, the building was 230 feet long by 33 feet wide.

On the roof, there was a bell turret and it was the ringing of the bell each Friday morning at 11 am which signalled the start of trading. Unfortunately, so fearful were local traders of competition that they determined that no one who had not served an apprenticeship of seven years in the trade should be allowed to sell goods in the Hall – or within a 10-mile radius of it. Perhaps not surprisingly, this restriction led to traders taking their goods to markets in other towns such as Bradford and Halifax and so the market in tammies in Wakefield declined rapidly, forcing the leasing of the hall for use as a warehouse, then a mill, for the production of worsted goods until 1863.

In 1851, there had been held in London, at the Crystal Palace, The Great Exhibition, where manufacturers had displayed their very latest technological goods developed in the heat of the industrial revolution.

Wakefield companies had taken part and some years later it was decided that the town should proceed to hold its own exhibition and a committee was established to this effect. They negotiated the rent of the Tammy Hall for use of the Wakefield Industrial and Fine Art Exhibition which was to run from 30th August to 19th October 1865, but not until the Hall had been extended to the front with a glass and timber exhibition hall. Records show that 189,423 people visited at an average of 4,735 visitors per day, peaking at over 10,000 visitors on 7th October. Profits from the exhibition were used to found what is now Wakefield College.

After the exhibition, the Hall was sold to Wakefield Corporation who demolished one end of it to create a building site for their new Town Hall. They then modified the remaining part of the building to convert it into a police and fire station, opening in 1878. Although the building had been reduced in length, it had doubled in width and a new house was incorporated for the chief of the Wakefield police.

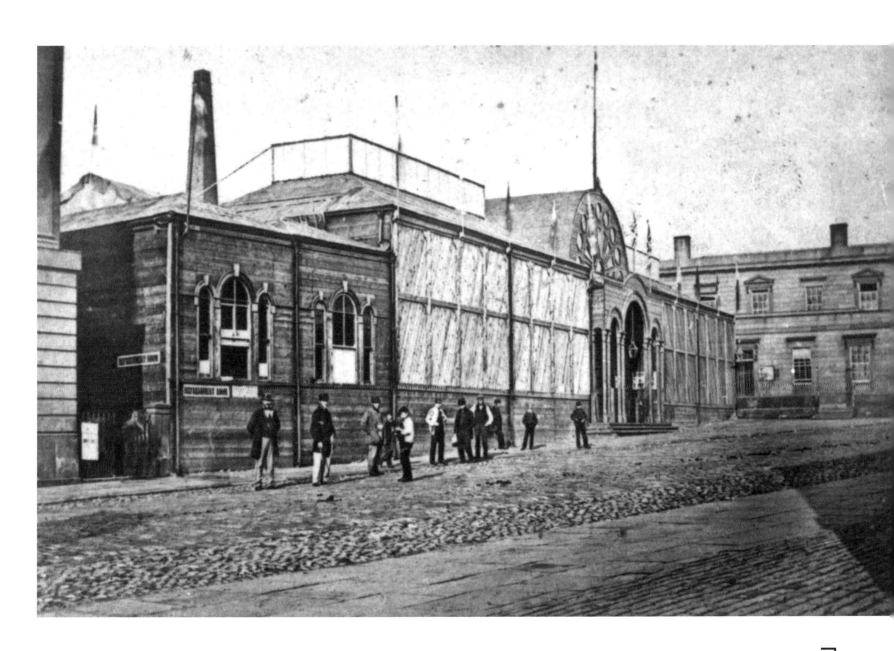

Tammy Hall showing the glass exhibition hall used for the Wakefield Industrial and Fine Art Exhibition of 1865. Photo courtesy of the RG Pearson Collection

Wakefield Industrial & Fine Art Exhibition 1865

Tammy Hall as painted in a watercolour by architect William Watson and used to illustrate the exhibition catalogue. The artist appears to have taken certain liberties with perspective here to aggrandise the scale of the building! Image courtesy of Brian Holding

At some point, the garage for the fire engine was extended and changes made to the building. As can been seen from the photos below and overleaf, there were two doors for vehicles to the King Street end in addition to the single entrance on the other side.

Further changes were made when these twin entries onto King Street were blocked off, and the front window of the house re-instated – although it retained the curved arch over the top rather than the pedimented window style that had existed before (see photos overleaf).

The building had 19 cells to hold prisoners pending trial and prisoners could be taken to the courtroom in the Town Hall via a tunnel under Gill Street.

The building eventually became the Magistrates Courts, a function it retained until 2016 when the Courts moved to Leeds.

Photos on this page, courtesy of Wakefield Council, show changes made to the King Street elevation of Tammy Hall

Tammy Hall today: some of the original cells were retained during the time when the building was used as the Magistrates Court

The Mechanics' Institution

Originally built in 1820-23 as Public Rooms with a music salon on the first floor, the building also contained a subscription library, a newsroom, a savings bank and, in the basement, a dispensary with accommodation for an apothecary and two servants. The architect was Charles Watson again.

The Mechanics' Institution leased the building from 1841 and bought it outright in 1855, thereby forestalling Wakefield Corporation from purchasing it to use as a Town Hall.

In 1910, the building was re-named The Institute of Literature and Science. In 1935, the building was offered to the Council who acquired it in 1936. From 1955 until 2012, it was used as the City's museum.

The museum moved to the Council's new civic building, Wakefield One, in 2013 and the Mechanics' Institution was leased to Wakefield College who completed a major refurbishment and conversion to create a new centre for performing arts.

With class rooms and rehearsal rooms on the ground floor and in the basement, the building is now called The Waterton Building within the College estate, after Wakefield naturalist Charles Waterton of Walton Hall whose collection of exotic wildlife was displayed here in the museum for many years (a selection is now on display at the new museum in Wakefield One).

Upstairs on the first floor, the building now features a new theatre, the Mechanics' Theatre, which can accommodate over 150 people. The building is Grade II* listed.

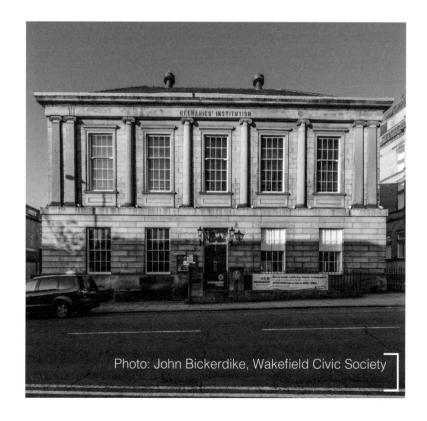

Photo: John Bickerdike, Wakefield Civic Society

Banking

The banking firm of Leatham, Tew and Co was originally established in Doncaster and Pontefract in 1801. In 1809, the bank acquired premises in Wakefield when it took over the failing Wakefield firm of Ingram, Kennett and Ingram and opened a branch on the corner of Wood Street and Silver Street. This was at a time when there were many small and independently-owned banks.

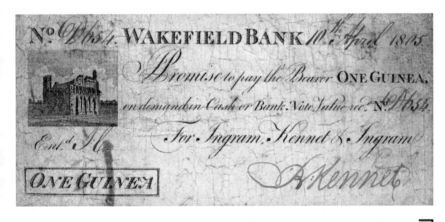

Ingram, Kennet and Ingram bank note for one guinea and featuring a picture of the Chantry Chapel. Photo: – Wakefield Council Libraries Photographic Collection

In 1880, the bank commissioned the building of imposing new premises, designed for them by Leeds architects J Neill and Son. This new building, still on the Wood Street site, opened to customers in 1881. It's actually two buildings: look at the Wood Street elevation and you'll notice the main banking hall to the left and then a smaller version to the right, known as Bank House.

This smaller building was designed as residential accommodation for the bank manager. In fact, there was further accommodation for staff provided on the first floor above the banking hall. (Notice the dates 1809 and 1881 inscribed above the windows representing the year the company was established in Wakefield and the year the new building opened.)

Leatham, Tew and Co continued in existence as an independent bank until their merger with Barclays Bank in 1906. The premises on the corner of Wood Street remained in use as a bank until Barclays moved to Trinity Walk in 2012, ending a banking tradition on the site that had endured for over two centuries.

After a period of around four years during which the condition of the building deteriorated, it was purchased by Matthew and Jenny Burton, owners of the Qubana Restaurant in Northgate. They began work to convert the old bank into a stylish bar and restaurant, opening for business in early 2017 and transferring the Qubana name to their new premises. The project was awarded a Wakefield Civic Society Design Award in April 2017.

The bank of Townend and Rishworth was founded in 1802 by Thomas Rishworth, formerly the senior clerk at Ingram's, and a Mr Townend of York. Following a run on the bank, it was forced to merge with a York bank in 1812 to become Wentworth, Chaloner and Rishworth. When this too failed in 1825, the Rishworth family were forced to sell Rishworth House, the site of today's County Hall.

1-3 Wood Street – formerly Barclays Bank and now Qubana Restaurant. Photo: John Bickerdike, Wakefield Civic Society

Cross Street and Radcliffe Place

Once upon a time – in fact, until the 1960s, Cross Street, which links Northgate with Wood Street, took a rather more twisting route than it does today. As the map, right, from 1893 shows, there was a distinct dog-leg twist to the layout of the street.

The street was eventually straightened out in the 1960s when some of the buildings in Wood Street were demolished. The illustration opposite shows how these buildings used to look. The round-ended building was, in fact, a post office and you can just about make out the post box built into the wall to the right-hand side of the doorway.

That post box was dated 1809 and still exists in the collections of Wakefield Museum and is believed to be the oldest surviving post box in the country.

Note the railings and trees to the left of centre in the picture. These mark the boundary of an earlier Clayton Hospital and Dispensary.

The first public dispensary dates from 1787 when a house in Northgate near its junction with Kirkgate was used for the purpose and funded by subscription and a grant of £30 a year from the Overseers of the Poor.

The house was demolished in the 1820s and the dispensary moved into the basement of the Public Rooms in Wood Street (the building that was later to become the Mechanics' Institution).

Taken from a 1893 map held in Wakefield Local Studies Library at Wakefield One

The 1809 post box from Wood Street post office. Courtesy of Wakefield Council

A black and white print from the Henry Clarke collection showing the junction of Cross Street (left) and Wood Street (on the right). To the left of the curved end building ran Post Office Yard. The name of this was later changed to Radcliffe Place when the Radcliffe print works were established in the yard by George Radcliffe, whose son John (1650-1714) went on to become royal physician to William and Mary. The trees are in the garden of Clayton Hospital.
Illustration: Wakefield Libraries Photographic Collection.

Following the death of the apothecary, who lived in the basement of the Public Rooms and in conditions that were regarded as damp and unhealthy, the dispensary moved to a house in Barstow Square. In 1854, the dispensary was relocated to a house in Wood Street. A gift from Wakefield businessman Thomas Clayton enabled the building of wards and later a new wing, the Albert Wing, in memory of Prince Albert who died in December 1861. The name of the dispensary was changed to Clayton Hospital and Dispensary.

When Clayton died in 1868, he left half of his estate to the hospital and this enabled the building of a new hospital between Northgate and Wentworth Street. Meanwhile, the former building in Wood Street was, with the addition of another floor, converted into offices, known as City Chambers, and this continued in use until its demolition in 1973. Meanwhile, new offices and shops, styled New City Chambers, were built in front of the old hospital building, at the corner of Wood Street and Cross Street.

The original Clayton Hospital and Dispensary on Wood Street.
Photo: Yorkshire Archaeological and History Society

New City Chambers on the corner of Wood Street and Cross Street. The first three bays on Cross Street were built first, in the garden in front of the old hospital. Going down Cross Street, the next building on the left is Cross Street Chambers and this stands on the site of the old hospital

Victoria Chambers

This building is a bit of a mystery. It stands on the site of a former aerated water company. Chambers Trade Directory of 1901 shows that the site was being used by someone by the name of Moorhouse who was a chemist, druggist and mineral water manufacturer. But does that refer to this rather grand building or one that came earlier?

Look up at the gables on the front of this building and you will see two dates – 1863 and 1905. To what could they refer?

Well, a stone plaque on the ground floor inside the building bears an inscription that tells us the plaque was laid by the directors of the Yorkshire Waggon Company on 4th May 1905. The company was established in 1863 and originally operated from Barstow Square (although their factory was near Horbury railway station). According to Grace's Guide to British Industrial History (available on-line), the Wood Street building was called Yorkshire Buildings when first erected. This all suggests that the building we see today was built for the company in 1905.

Kelly's Directory shows the building was still called Yorkshire Buildings in1927 and was still home to the Yorkshire Waggon Company along with a number of other businesses. But how did it acquire its current name? Well, it appears that the new name came about when the building became the offices of the Liverpool Victoria Insurance Company in the latter part of the 20th century.

Today, the building has been refurbished inside as offices to let and is home to a number of different businesses.

This part of the former Wood Street Police Station, photographed here by John Bickerdike of Wakefield Civic Society, was originally built as health offices for the West Riding County Council in 1931. They stand on the site of the Paragon Iron Works which were demolished by 1910 – see page 12 for a comparison.

Three Police Stations

The town of Wakefield acquired its first police force in 1848 with incorporation (see page 13) and the creation of Wakefield Corporation. Before that, order had been maintained by the Manor's constables. The new force took over the building in King Street which had been used since the 1820s by the constables and which still stands today (at 14a King Street, top right) although now converted into offices but retaining the original cell door. The town's fire engine was also kept here from 1829. The police and fire station moved to the Tammy Hall after it was converted in 1878 (see page 21).

Meanwhile, the county police force, set up in 1842 (with 10 constables), was having to make do with an office and cells in the Court House on Wood Street – an arrangement that was less than ideal. In 1908-09, a new police station was built for the Lower Agbrigg Constabulary (bottom right), opposite the Town Hall.

This new building was built on the site of the by then demolished Royal Hotel (previously The Woodman Inn). It was designed by Vickers Edwards, and built by George Crook, a local man who had bought the Westgate Brick Company.

With local government re-organisation in the 1970s, the police were able to extend into the offices next door which had been built in 1931 to a design by P O Platts for the Medical Officer of Health. These offices, pictured left, were themselves built on the site of an iron foundry, the Paragon Works.

A Centre for Retail and Leisure

Today, there are bars and restaurants along Wood Street and in surrounding streets close by – in fact, it seems, an ever increasing number of such establishments are opening in the area.

In Wood Street itself, there is the newly converted Barclays Bank building, now the Qubana Restaurant, and Damelio, a wine, cocktail and deli bar which opened in 2016. The latter was formerly Barristers and before that, The Chancery (often referred to as 'The Chance' locally). Although this building at 22 Wood Street dates from the 1930s, it stands on the site of the former Angel Inn which had been there since at least 1822. Could this Angel Inn have an ancestor, the Angel Inn that the Rev Wood demolished to open up the street in 1806? (See page 9)

Anyone trying to do research into the history of a street has a number of problems to contend with, not least of which is a tendency for people and businesses to move around and this is compounded when properties are renumbered over time, as seems to have happened in Wood Street. Space doesn't permit a full account of all the businesses and residents who occupied the street over the years, so what follows can only be an indication of what the Heart of Wakefield Project has so far uncovered.

Starting at 1-3 Wood Street, now Qubana, the first shop we encounter is no. 5 Wood Street, although this was originally no. 3, possibly because Bank House (page 27), having a name, did not at first have a number.

The 1927 Kelly's Directory lists the following firms on Wood Street (west side – i.e., up from Barclays Bank):

No. 5 – Charles Turner and Son, house decorators (see photo right)

No. 7 – John Crockatt Ltd, dyers (note that the photo of Turners seems to indicate that Crockatt was at one time to the left of Turner's shop – Kelly's Directory for 1892 confirms this to be so – but why did they swap?)

No. 9 – John Walter Watson, hatter

No. 11 – John Dickinson and Son, solicitors

No. 13 – James Holdsworth, ironmonger (property now rebuilt as Holdsworth House)

No. 15 – Kay and Lunan, architects (formerly the Mexboro Arms)

No. 15 – Madam Millicent Hayes, milliner

No. 17 – William Braham, hosier

Hyland Ltd, auto engineers occupied the remaining buildings up to Chancery Lane. Known as Hyland Buildings they were home to a number of businesses – an estate agent, ladies hairdressers, chiropodist, and a Christian Science Reading Room. Hylands were perhaps unusual for a city centre shop as they sold not only cars but also sea-going motor cruisers – as their advertisement from the 1930s reproduced opposite shows.

In the 1930s, no.9 had become Bon Marché, a ladies' outfitters. Records show that no.11, was occupied in the 1880s by Harry Wood, professor of music. The 1901 census shows the occupant to be Kate Wood, a widow, who taught music and dealt in pianofortes. Could there have been a connection with the Woods Music Shop that later occupied the corner plot of Wood Street and Cross Square?

In 1927 the buildings on the east side of the street started at No. 2 with William Henry Dyson, wine and spirit merchant. Dyson seems to have taken over the business from a John Jones in between the compilation of the 1887 and 1888 Kelly Directories. Dyson's continued until at least the 1960s but by 1971, the shop had become Lavell's newsagents. Today, it is home to William Brown, the estate agent.

One shop that needs special mention on this side of the street is the former Eagle Press that stood at No.18 for many years until it closed in 2008. Not only printers and stationers, they sold artists' materials, books, maps and, most importantly for a young boy at the time, train sets and other toys! The shop closed and the property is now a restaurant.

Space permits just one final mention. The last shop in the row, after Cross Street had been straightened out and the end buildings demolished, was a photography shop. When this fell empty in 1968 before it too was demolished and the site redeveloped, Wakefield Civic Society took over the shop for an exhibition - the photo below, centre, from the Society's collection, shows committee members getting things ready.

Turner's shop in Wood Street. Photo courtesy of Wakefield Council

George and Crown Yard

This yard, which runs parallel with Wood Street to the west, is actually older than Wood Street itself (look at the Enclosures map on page 10). It takes its name from the George and Crown Inn that stood up the yard on the left until it was demolished in 1858 (see JW Walker). The yard leads up from Silver Street to Crown Court, the location of the Assembly Rooms that were to become the first Town Hall, while the 'new' Town Hall lies directly ahead. Along the length of the yard, you will see former warehouses, now pubs, and the old Auction Rooms, now converted into offices.

As Wakefield developed as a market town and inland port (the river is navigable to both the east and west coasts via the canal system), warehouses became commonplace in the many yards emanating from the principal streets.

The illustration right, from a watercolour by Roger Brown of Wakefield Civic Society and based on a drawing by Henry Clarke, depicts the Yard in the 1880s. The building in the foreground on the left of the Yard was, at the time, Loveday's, a jewellers and silversmiths. It was built, with a house behind on the site of the George and Crown Inn by Mr Loveday. The screens hanging from the windows are actually reflectors, intended to bring as much light as possible into the workshops at the rear of the property.

The shop has been used for a number of business purposes over the years. For example, Kelly's Directory for Wakefield shows that it was occupied by Summers and Co. a drapery firm in the 1920s. It has also been used as a wine retailers and a furniture store (Jays, later Woodhouse) and was more recently used as an amusement arcade for a number of years. In early 2017, after a period of disuse, it was being refurbished and converted into student accommodation above and commercial use at ground level.

The photo to the right was taken in 1964 when buildings along Silver Street and Marygate were being demolished in preparation for new development. On the right of the picture is the former Loveday's jewellery shop seen in the illustration on page 37 opposite. The white building in the centre of the photograph is thought to date from the 17th century.

The jettied architectural style (where upper floors project beyond the floors below) is typical of the period and would have been a common sight at one time.

There are shops on the ground floor while the door to the right of the building leads through to the Black Swan Yard where can be found the Black Swan public house at the back. The whole building is listed Grade II.

Photo courtesy Wakefield Council Libraries Photographic Collection

Wood Street Closed!

There have been many occasions when Wood Street has been closed to traffic for royal visits, civic, military, and remembrance parades and miners' galas. Here are just a couple of the more unusual occasions when the street has been closed in recent times.

Wood Street Markets (top right):

As well as being used for civic and other parades, Wood Street is occasionally closed to traffic for special events. One such occasion occurred during the summer of 2013 when, following an initiative from architect Darren Bailey, local businesses and other organisations, including Wakefield Council and Wakefield Civic Society, worked together to stage three weekend markets. In December of the same year, 'Wood Street' Market went on tour when it opened up at Merchant Gate for a weekend.

The Green comes to Wood Street (bottom right):

Over three days, from 10th to 12th October 2003, Wakefield–based charity Public Arts (now operating as Beam), transformed Wood Street in a project intended to get people talking about how to make the best use of open spaces – should they be given over to cars or reclaimed for pedestrians to enjoy? Co-designed by artist Walter Jack and landscape architects Whitelaw Turkington, The Green: The Yorkshire Festival of Places appeared over five consecutive weekends in Bridlington, Huddersfield, Halifax, Doncaster and Wakefield.

Photo credit: Grenville Charles, courtesy of Beam

The Future of Wood Street

As we have seen, ever since Wood Street was first laid out in the early 19th century, the street has evolved. Buildings have gone up, been changed and demolished. People and businesses have moved in and moved out. Such changes are inevitable in any street but particularly one at the heart of a city. At the time of writing this book, it seems clear that Wood Street is about to enter a new phase in its history.

Two prominent buildings lie empty – the Old Court House, currently wrapped in plastic and surrounded by scaffolding is awaiting repairs but needs a new purpose. The former police station has been vacated and is similarly looking for a new use. At one time, the Court building was going to be turned into a gallery and restaurant but the developer failed to deliver the project and, after a long period where the building was allowed to deteriorate, Wakefield Council stepped in to rescue the building. The Council have also bought the former police station, no doubt to prevent a repetition of the problems experienced with the Court House. There is talk of the police station being turned into a hotel, which would certainly help to revitalise the street.

Whatever the specific outcomes for these two buildings (and the former Magistrates Court – the old Tammy Hall – also empty since the end of 2016), we know that the Council is working on a regeneration plan for the 'Civic Quarter' which could see some significant changes to the area around and along Wood Street.

The Rishworth Street multi-storey car park is scheduled for demolition along with some other buildings in Gills Yard (behind the former police station); there is potential for new development in Northgate and the Merchant Gate development near to Westgate Station will bring new business and residents to the vicinity, all of which could help to bring new life back to Wood Street.

Wakefield College continues to develop its City Centre Campus – existing buildings are being refurbished and modernised and the new Advanced Skills and Learning Centre is nearing completion as the College works towards becoming a university centre. Although some of the shops in the street have lain empty for too long, new businesses are moving into the street. Meanwhile, space above shops is being converted into living accommodation, bringing a new resident population into the street. Long-established restaurants and bars in and around Wood Street are now being joined by new ventures opening up in the area.

All this is a demonstration of the growing confidence in the city. Wood Street and its neighbours will soon once again have every claim to being the beating Heart of Wakefield.

The Protection of our built heritage – The Wood Street Conservation Area

Wood Street sits at the centre of the Wood Street Conservation Area. There are 29 Conservation Areas across the Wakefield Metropolitan District Council area, of which 8 are in the city centre: St John's, Wentworth Terrace, Wood Street, Cathedral, Upper Westgate, Lower Westgate, South Parade and the Waterfront. (Details of Wakefield's Conservation Areas, including maps, can be downloaded from the website of Wakefield Council).

Conservation Areas are specially designated areas of land and property with specific architectural or historic interest. They are designated to protect and enhance those qualities and characteristics that make them special by placing an extra tier of planning control on any new development or alterations and demolition. These controls can relate to both the built and the natural environment within a Conservation Area so as to protect the character of the area. This means, for example, that additional scrutiny will be given to planning applications within a Conservation Area in terms of not only the visual impact of any changes but also in terms of the materials that might be used. Local authorities are usually responsible for designating Conservation Areas and for taking any enforcement action required where developers or property owners are judged to be in breach of planning policies or are judged to have introduced discordant elements into a Conservation Area.

So, local authorities will check that any proposed development within or likely to affect a Conservation Area will not have an adverse effect on:

- open spaces, views, landmarks and landscape that contribute to their character, appearance or setting;
- the character of any buildings or structures having regard to local scale, proportion, details and materials;
- the preservation of features of architectural, archaeological and historic interest.

A Conservation Area designation does not prevent development nor does it remove certain permitted development rights. However, where owners individually make a series of what might be small-scale changes to their properties, the cumulative impact could erode the special qualities of the Conservation Area. To prevent this, a local authority can make an 'Article 4 Direction' under the Town and Country Planning Act (General Permitted Development) Order 1995. This has the effect of removing permitted development rights.

Conservation Areas were first introduced into the UK under the 1967 Civic Amenities Act and some of the first to be designated in this region were in Wakefield – at St John's and South Parade. Others were in York, Huddersfield and Thorne near Doncaster. There are now 875 Conservation Areas within Yorkshire and some 10,000 across the UK.

Conservation Areas are just one of several designations that can be used to protect our 'heritage assets'. Other designations can be national or local and include, for example, Scheduled Ancient Monuments, Listed Buildings and Buildings of Local Interest. Some designations, such as Ramsar Sites (which protect wetlands) and Marine Protected Areas, are international designations. Listed building status usually means that no structural changes can be made without first obtaining listed building consent from the local authority.

Although 2017 is the 50th anniversary of Conservation Areas in the UK, we were not the first to implement them! The earliest 'Conservation Areas' were introduced in the "Vieux Carré", or French Quarter, of New Orleans in 1921, followed by Charleston (1930), Salem (1936) & Georgetown (1950). Czechoslovakia designated 50 urban conservation sites in 1950. And France instituted "Secteurs Sauvegardés" in 1962.

The Wood Street Conservation Area in width stretches from King Street (east side – the west side is in the Upper Westgate Conservation Area), across Wood Street, to Radcliffe Place and Gills Yard. In length, it reaches from the top side of County Hall down to the junction of Wood Street with Cross Square and the Bull Ring. However, it does not include the former Barclays Bank (now Qubana) building which instead falls into the Upper Westgate Conservation Area.

The Town and County Halls are listed buildings, designated Grade I – the highest level of listing protection. The Old Court House and Mechanics' Institution are listed Grade II*, while the Old Town Hall, No. 1 Tammy Hall Street, Nos. 6 & 8 Silver Street (the Black Swan public house), Nos. 2-8 Castrop-Rauxel Square and the red telephone box outside the Old Court House are all listed Grade II, as are 49 King Street and Bank House (the solicitors' offices on the corner of Burton Street and Cliff Parade, which additionally sit within this Conservation Area although outside the scope of this book.

You can find out more about the protection of historic assets on the Historic England website.

Acknowledgements and Picture Credits

There are a number of individuals who have directly, or indirectly, contributed to the writing and production of this book.

In particular, I would like to acknowledge the help provided by Pam Judkins and Dr Phil Judkins of Wakefield Historical Society whose knowledge of the history of Wakefield has been invaluable.

Unless stated, photos used in this book are those of the Author but thanks are due to the following individuals and organisations for their help and permission to use photos and other images: John Bickerdike, Roger Brown, and Brian Holding. Thanks also to Lesley Taylor for tracking down the image of the Enclosures Map used on page 10 from West Yorkshire Archive Service who gave permission to use it.

Other photos and illustrations have been reproduced with the kind permission of Wakefield Council and Wakefield Libraries Photographic Collection, The Francis Frith Collection, and Mrs S Edwards for the RG Pearson Collection.

Special thanks also to Faceless Arts and the people of Wakefield who engaged with the project to create original artwork, some of which has been reproduced in this book.

Others who deserve mention for their help include the volunteers of the Heart of Wakefield Project not already mentioned who have contributed to the ongoing research for the project, Craig Broadwith of Historic England for some of the information on Conservation Areas in the UK and abroad included on page 42.

Wakefield Council Creative Services for their help with the design and layout of the book.

Mike O'Donnell, Secretary of Wakefield Civic Society, for proof-reading the final draft and correcting my typing and Jean Broadbent, the Civic Society's Treasurer, for arranging for a group of project members to visit to the former Magistrates Court (Tammy Hall) to make a photographic record of the interior.

And finally, thank you to my partner Brian Ward for providing the many cups of coffee that have sustained me through the hours spent writing this book.

Further Reading

There is a growing body of work in which the story of Wakefield is told through research-based text, historic photographs, paintings, drawings, and oral histories. My own bookshelves are slowly being weighed down as my own collection of books about Wakefield grows

Now it is my turn to add to that list of books but, in so doing I must pay tribute to the work that has been done by others, particularly historians such as JW Walker, John Goodchild and Kate Taylor, and members of Wakefield Historical Society who have written various essays and books over the years.

What is original in this book is the arrangement of the content – to focus on just one of Wakefield's principal streets to provide a guide that will appeal to anyone wishing to explore. However, the serious student will want to turn to other works, as I have done, for more detailed analysis on the city's wider history and development.

With this in mind, I commend the books listed below – not all of them are in print, alas, but they can often be picked up second-hand and are, of course, available in the Wakefield One Library.

Reading List:
JW Walker, 1934, *Wakefield Its History and People*, The West Yorkshire Printing Co. (Later republished in a two-volume third edition in 1966 by S.R Publishers Ltd.)

John Goodchild, 1986, *Attorney at Large – the Concerns of John Lee of Wakefield 1759-1836*, Wakefield Historical Publications

Kate Taylor, 2008, *The Making of Wakefield 1801-1900*, Wharncliffe Books

Anne Barnes, *Cheaper by the Yard: Wakefield Yards*, published in *Aspects of Wakefield*, *(Volume 3)*, Edited by Kate Taylor, 2001, Wharncliffe Books

Wakefield Civic Society

Wakefield Civic Society - an organisation dedicated to making Wakefield a better place in which to live, work or relax.

Whether you are a resident or a visitor to Wakefield, the Society can offer something of interest. We run a full programme of events throughout the year. From talks and social events to guided walks and excursions, there is something for everyone

Our members receive regular updates on what is happening in Wakefield and have opportunities to take part in the debate on how Wakefield develops. The Society was established in 1964 out of a concern for the built environment of our city. As a registered charity (number 236034), the Society is dedicated both to preserving and celebrating our built heritage and to campaigning for new developments to be of the very highest standard and quality possible. We regularly scrutinise planning applications submitted to the council and raise comments where we consider it appropriate to do so. We also discuss proposals for new developments with property owners, developers and council officials in order to help improve outcomes.

We run an annual design awards scheme where we recognise the very best in architectural and environmental projects whether they be for new buildings or refurbishment of older ones. Winners are presented with one of our brass plaques while runners up receive commendations.

We also run a blue plaques scheme where plaques are erected to commemorate the life of an individual associated with the city or to mark the history of a building of local interest. Plaques can also be considered for significant events that have occurred in and around Wakefield.

As a charity, the Society depends principally for its income on the annual subscriptions it receives from its members and on donations received from members of the public and we offer a range of personal and corporate memberships. To find out more about the work of the Society and how you can help us, please visit our website www.wakefieldcivicsociety.org.uk or follow us on Twitter @WakefieldCivicS.

The Society is run by a committee of elected volunteers who receive no remuneration for their work.

Wakefield Civic Society is a member of both Civic Voice and YHACS.